STRETCH
Marks

STRETCH Marks

"how to grow beyond your limits"

Laticia J. Norton

XULON PRESS

Xulon Press
2301 Lucien Way #415
Maitland, FL 32751
407.339.4217
www.xulonpress.com

© 2020 by Laticia J. Norton

All rights reserved solely by the author. The author guarantees all contents are original and do not infringe upon the legal rights of any other person or work. No part of this book may be reproduced in any form without the permission of the author. The views expressed in this book are not necessarily those of the publisher.

Unless otherwise indicated, Scripture quotations taken from the Holy Bible, New International Version (NIV). Copyright © 1973, 1978, 1984, 2011 by Biblica, Inc.™. Used by permission. All rights reserved.

Scripture quotations taken from the King James Version (KJV)–*public domain.*

Scripture quotations taken from the Holy Bible, New Living Translation (NLT). Copyright ©1996, 2004, 2007 by Tyndale House Foundation. Used by permission of Tyndale House Publishers, Inc.

Printed in the United States of America.

ISBN-13: 978-1-6312-9095-4

DEDICATION

I want to dedicate this book to my inspiration for all that I set out to accomplish in life, my amazing children Taj, Tysen and Taraji. You have been my why from day one and I am forever grateful that God gave me you.

FOREWARD

I thought that I had reached my limits. I thought that I had grown as much as I could grow. Then I began to experience life in more ways than I could imagine. I felt like I was being pulled. Each time I felt the tightness of my existence expand, more, and more, and more, and more. Extension was inevitable. I had been stretched and I had the marks to prove it!

If you are seeking an explanation as to why it had to be you to go through what your going through. If you feel as though you just can't take anymore then this book will help you understand how to grow beyond your limits and into God's purpose for your life. In this walk with God, we must understand that we will be stretched to capacity by the situations and circumstances of life. When this occurs, it is then that God steps in and becomes the elastic that allows us to be able to expand, adapt, change, and recover. God does this just for us, but not without leaving marks. The marks are the reminders that it is you, you are real, and you are still here, alive, growing and becoming. The marks are for those that need to see it to believe it. In (John 20:27), Jesus instructed Thomas to touch his hand and his side to feel the marks, so that he may believe.

Shereeta Black

TABLE OF CONTENTS

Dedication v
Foreward vii
Introduction. xi
Change Your Now 1
Find Your Inner Fight. 4
Use Your Passion To Fulfill Your Purpose 7
Have Some Integrity About Yourself. 13
Lead By Example 15
Burying Money Won't Grow A Tree 17
Be Silent And Listen. 21
The 3 D's You Must Avoid 25
Subduing Narcissistic Characteristics 28
G.O.A.L.S./ Greatness On All Levels: Strive for it! 34
Excellence Is The Only Standard! 37
Utilize Your Resources 41
Dedicate Yourself To God. 44
Don't Be A Statistic 48
Your Authenticity Requires Your Accountability 53
The Truth Will Make You Free!. 57
Don't Be Scared 60
Believing Is Seeing 65
Don't Let Frustration Cause You To Quit. 68
For All Intents And Purposes 72
Keep Up Or Get Left Behind. 76

INTRODUCTION

My incredibly wise and strikingly handsome husband sent me a message one day to encourage me because I was having a rough day and frankly, I was ready to quit on my vision. He said to me:

> The moment we breakdown isn't a break-down from our failures. We're breaking down because the renewed us is awake and our old life isn't enough and sometimes that's the reason we seem to not know what to do... but mentally we are blocked by our old thoughts which in return makes us afraid of the moves we know we have to make and the steps we must take because the renewed you needs this but our old ways of thinking can sometimes kill the renewed you before we can even hit the ground running.

It was just the thing I needed to hear to lift my spirits. I wrote a song titled "Activated" that says: "You've been studying in silence, seeking and praying, watching in private and you didn't even know why. You've been hungry for things that you don't understand but it was for this moment please let me explain... you've been activated."

The lyrics to this song describes the details of the actions that take place when you have been awakened. At first, it's foreign to you, almost as if your feelings are happening to the wrong person. However, if this has been you at any point, then you are the right person to be feeling what you're feeling. God doesn't make mistakes. He has been preparing you for some time now. God has given you vision, ability, and purpose. Yet, this new feeling is called hunger. You become activated when you begin to feel starvation and real hunger strikes.

In the natural sense, we have all experienced what it feels like to be hungry, but I don't think we know what it feels like to be *starving*. Starvation brings with it other feelings, such as pain. I don't know about you but when I get really hungry, my stomach begins to hurt. That is synonymous to the pain of feeling stuck in the same place in life, wanting to move forward but not knowing how. It also brings weakness and fatigue. You can't muster up the strength or energy to do anything. You're tired of the same routine, but too weak to try anything different because you have become complacent where you are, or you don't know enough to make a move, which feels like too much work to learn. The last thing it can bring is death—in extreme cases where hunger turns into starvation and is left unattended for too long, death is inevitable.

Now, this is the same in any sense you look at it. Death means the end. Yet, the beautiful thing about some types of death is that some things must die in order for other things to live.

Your purpose will never be dead as long as there is breath in your lungs.

We just have to learn how to resuscitate our unconscious purpose. Just as we go through these things naturally, we also experience them spiritually. Hunger in the spirit is equivalent to the level hunger we feel in the flesh when desperation kicks in. It's that final attempt at self-preservation before hunger turns into starvation. At this stage, we find a supernatural strength that allows us to fight harder than we ever have before to, well, live.

I want to speak to the hungry you—the one willing to put up the valiant effort to fight for the vision and the purpose that God has placed inside of you. I want to speak to that version of you because that is the you that is most receptive and willing to push toward destiny. As you read, I want your undivided attention—not to me, but to the details that apply to your life and your spiritual growth and advancement. The gems and nuggets are strategically placed by the Holy Spirit throughout this written work. I'm going to take this time to admonish you to take notes and put it in your own words so it becomes relevant to your daily life and easy to apply.

Also, don't think you will get all of the key points and applicable treasures in just one read. You will need to go back and reread the chapters that connect with your situation as you are walking it out. Then, you will begin to see the pages come to life right before your eyes. Don't be afraid to highlight what sticks out to you.

Lastly, I want to ask you to proceed with an open mind, ready to receive all that this literary composition has to offer. I pray the wisdom that unfolds on each page brings you as much joy to read as it did for me to write. Happy reading!

Chapter 1

CHANGE YOUR NOW

And change it *right now*.

Notice I didn't say, "God, change my now." That's because God has given us the power to declare some things over ourselves and change happens to be one of them. In order for us, as children of God, to receive all that God has for us, there are parts of our current situation that have to change. This chapter is going to be leaning toward the spiritual side than the natural. The reason for that is simply we are naturally spiritual beings and when the spirit of a man accepts change, it is evident in the natural realm as it pertains to how we view and respond to what happens to us.

Take a look in the mirror. Where you are in your life is in direct response to the decisions that that person looking back at you has made. So don't blame others. Take responsibility for you. The greatest thing about your life is that you can't change your destiny with one step because it is predestined for you to succeed—even if you don't yet know it—but you can change your direction. Put your best foot forward today. You were born for greatness!

In order to tap into the power that we have on the inside of us to promote change, we need to first surrender to the will of God.

I heard a songwriter say, "The change I want to see must first begin in me, I surrender so your world can be changed." What that means is we have to grow to inspire growth in others. We are the light that others need.

You mean my actions may directly affect others? Yes! In fact, "may" isn't the right word; they will definitely affect others.

The Bible teaches us that we are to be vessels that reflect the light of our Father, being careful not to dim it, but let it shine bright for all to see, because in some cases, we may be the only light that others will see.

I know you're probably wondering, "What does my light shining to help others have to do with my change to better myself?" Everything, because the Bible also says you "shall reap what you sow" and the same level of concern you have for others is the same level of concern that will be returned to you. We are helpers one to another and if you can't do your part to be a help to others, how can you have any expectation of help being extended to you in your time of need?

Perception refers to how we view things in our current state or situation. Imagine three of you standing in a single file line, with five feet between the first you and the second you, and twenty feet between the second you and the third you. The "present you" is in the middle. Imagine you have been in this spot for some time, and you can't quite reach your goal because the gap is too far apart. You begin to question God: "You said you were going to do this in my marriage, my ministry, my family, my business, but I just don't see it happening." You start telling yourself, "If God wanted me to be successful, I would be there by now," or, "Maybe this isn't the plan for my life." However, God is saying, "Look again, and this time instead of looking with your natural eyes, try looking with your spiritual eyes."

We are not looking at the other gap. The gap from where you used to be and where you are now. That gap is much larger than the one in front of you and if God was there through all of that, then He wouldn't leave you when you're so close to reaching your goal.

Could it be that while we are waiting for God to "fix our life", God is waiting for us to stand up, and "do the work"? God is waiting for some of us to say, "Change me, Lord. I may need my situation to change. I may need my circumstances to change, God, but please begin the work in me!" I believe your breakthrough begins at that exact moment.

I heard a wise woman, Dr. Nicky Collins, say, "If you don't change your now, your future will always look like your past." This statement has been proven over time to be the absolute truth. Nothing is going to get better for you until you acknowledge the things in you that are holding you back. In order to do this, you must stretch beyond your limits because change in most cases is difficult to adapt to, but you are ready. I can feel it!

Chapter 2

FIND YOUR INNER FIGHT

In order for you to find and tap into your inner fight, you must first know your *why*. Why fight? Only you have the answer to this for your fight to be unleashed. For one person, it may be that you have had a hard upbringing where success didn't feel like it was even an option, but then you saw a glimmer of light that made success that much more attainable.

For another, it may be that everything in your life has always come easy and you have never had to work for anything, so when it comes to grinding and getting it from the muscle, others who have had to do it the hard way their whole life don't respect you or believe you have it in you. Now that you have hit a rough patch, you just want to prove to yourself that you have what it takes to do the work.

Second, we must know for whom we are fighting. It can be to set an example for your children and to give them a better life, or to secure your own future, or maybe you are the glue that holds your entire family together and everyone connected to you is depending on you to succeed. Whatever the reason, it must be important enough to make you want to fight for it.

Now, like many of us have personally experienced, every fight isn't always an easy win. The word "fight" implies there is an opposer or an opposing force fighting against you. Time restraints, limited resources, lack of finances, minimal to no support from family and loved ones, not being fully knowledgeable about a subject—these are just a small number of oppositions that can affect your will to fight. The way that opposition works is by piling up one thing after another, but there is a secret to beating the opposer: put your issues in perspective from easy fix to hard fix and when you work to fix the things that are in your control, you will find the answer to one problem will eliminate another issue. For instance, if you find you lack knowledge about the thing you are pursuing, you can begin by doing research, and in so doing, you may possibly stumble across free resources, which could lead to networking with people that share your interests and may even want to invest in your new venture, therefore allowing you to pay for assistance that ultimately causes you to have more free time.

You may ask, "But where is the time to do the research coming from, because I can't see it?" I'm glad you asked! If you could subtract ten minutes a day from your TV time, ten minutes from social media surfing, and ten minutes from phone calls, you just accumulated thirty minutes for research. Sound easy? I doubt it, because it is easier to keep doing what you're doing and complain about the fact that what you're doing isn't working, rather than to change what you're doing to do something that will work. You can't do the right things a few times and think that it's supposed to equate to greatness because success doesn't come from what you do occasionally. It comes from what you do consistently.

We must fight diligently. In order to be diligent we must be intentional with everything we do, just as our Heavenly Father is with us. Proverbs 13:4 says, "the soul of the sluggard craves and gets nothing, while the soul of the diligent is richly supplied."

James 1:12 says, "Blessed is the man who remains steadfast under trial, for when he has stood the test he will receive the crown of life, which God has promised to those who love him."

Proverbs 12:24 says "The hand of the diligent will rule, while the slothful will be put to forced labor."

Galatians 6:9 reads, "And let us not grow weary of doing good, for in due season we will reap, if we do not give up."

Ecclesiastes 9:10 says, "Whatever your hand finds to do, do it with your might." Now, I'm not saying that this is going to be a piece of cake, but what I am saying is that if I was ever going to be motivated to move based on words, what better words to use than the words of God? God's Word holds power of the promise that can never be broken so we can lick the stamp and mail it on this one because it's final. So if you took the time to read and let the words in the Scriptures above sink in, you should be ready to turn up because the promise for diligent work is reaping a harvest, a richly supplied soul, and a crown of life. Now let's go take back what has been taken from us by force.

Chapter 3
USE YOUR PASSION TO FULFILL YOUR PURPOSE

In order to do this, we must know and understand three things: what is passion, what am I passionate about, and how do I channel my passion in connection with my purpose? The biblical definition for the word passion is to suffer or endure. Passion is what fuels the engine to your purpose. Look at it like this: you have to go to the grocery store to get dinner and you go out to your car, get in, close the door, put your seatbelt on, adjust your mirrors, but when you go to start the engine, it won't turn over. You try it again and again, and it doesn't start. Then you decide to look at the dashboard to see if there are any emergency lights on to tell you what might be wrong and at that moment, you see it. You realize the car has no gas in it, so it won't be starting up just by turning the key in the ignition. You have to get a gas can and get to the gas station, fill it up, and bring it back to put it in your car. Then you can trust your vehicle to do what it's supposed to do because you have done what is needed to ensure it runs the next time you turn the key in the ignition.

Like the trip to the gas station to get the fuel to fulfill the mission of going to the store, we sometimes allow our passion to burn out and we need to be refueled, or in our case, rejuvenated. We have to go to another source to reignite the passion in us that once burned bright.

Now don't feel bad if this is your story because the beautiful thing about this is that it can be reversed. There is one thing we must remember about a gas can: it can only hold so much gas so it's clearly not designed to fill your car up—it is just the amount needed for you to get your car to a gas station so you can fill up. This is the same in your life. People or things that reignite your passion are not meant to fill you up, but they are meant to get the fire going again just so you can make it to the filling station, which is faith in God and believing in yourself.

Now, we must address that passion is an amazing thing to have, but if it is misguided or misdirected, it can be damaging or in worst case scenarios, destructive to our purpose. We can—and oftentimes do—want things or even people in the worst way. If we use passion in this way or allow passion in itself to be our guide, it will most definitely lead you down the wrong path, which is where the biblical definition of "passion" comes in. We must be willing to dismiss our fleshy desires to allow the Holy Spirit to help guide our passion in fulfilling its purpose. This sometimes can feel like suffering because the battle between the flesh and the spirit is most certainly real and we many times find it hard to submit our will to that of a higher authority. Yet, we must endure the suffering to gain the reward.

Before we can address the issue of how we channel our passion, we must first deal with the realization that passion can die or run out. Some ways that we run out of "gas in our cars of passion," if you will, is that we take a lot of meaningless unnecessary trips and we go driving around without a necessary plan of action so we don't "waste gas", going in circles, and before we know it—the tank is empty. This is one of the more prevalent reasons why banks or lenders ask for at least a two-year business plan at minimum before they will consider investing. They are looking to see if you have an organized, logical plan of action that will have a high probability of success, which will give them a lower risk and greater odds of receiving a return on their investment. In all facets of life, the saying still reigns true that if you fail to plan, you plan to fail. Not so much because of a lack of ambition, but more so due to a lack of structure.

I have experienced this personally with my business. I came into my ownership excited and eager to make money moves that would grow my brand and take the venture to the next level. What I didn't come into my ownership with was knowledge and experience. At the time I was a professional stylist only, and if I knew anything, I knew hair. Yet, I didn't factor that running a business had little to do with the type of business that it was and all to do with structure, management, and teamwork. So needless to say, I began driving in circles and burning out all of my gas by my third year. Tension was high, stress was high, overhead was high, in fact the only thing that was low was my spirit. I felt like I was out of options and had exhausted all of my possibilities.

When I was ready to wave the white flag of defeat, I had a client come in and give me some advice that changed my life. It didn't happen overnight, but what it did was give me enough of a boost to get back up and try again. It also reminded me that I needed to pray and ask God, the one who had given me the business in the first place, to direct my next step and every step from that day forward. It was that unexpected "can of gas" that allowed me to make it back to the filling station.

The truth is that I have gone through this process more than once and as long as we have the ability to become exhausted, I can and possibly will go through it again, but there is nothing wrong with knowing that you need a jumpstart to get going again. In fact, the only thing that I see wrong about it is if you don't acknowledge when you need it so you can get what you need to keep going. This is so important for me to address because it is oftentimes the one thing that causes us to quit: we must acknowledge when we need help refocusing. This is prevalent in mothers because as a mom, we have a tendency to lose ourselves while we provide what everyone else needs. I want to take this section of the book to remind you that you are meant for more than what you settle for. Your dreams and aspirations are important and fulfilling them doesn't make you neglectful, no matter what you have been made to believe. This is why it is just as important to invest in your mental and emotional wellbeing as it is to invest in your financial wellbeing. There are mentoring programs and motivational workshops that are designed to awaken and fuel the you that you were always meant to be. Don't be another statistic or a "doubting Thomas" sitting on the sidelines watching others live the life that is accessible to you and meant for you because you were not willing to step outside of your comfort zone to try something you never tried before by allowing someone to help you get there.

Another way we burn unnecessary fuel is by allowing others to borrow our cars and returning them on E. We do understand there are partnerships and connections that need to be formed in order to grow and reach certain levels, but the problem with this is when you are willing to give so much of yourself (time, money, expertise, advice) to build a relationship with this particular individual and never get anything in return. It can cause you to feel used and drained. The key to preventing yourself from being found in this position is to thoroughly evaluate every situation and consult with a trusted advisor, if necessary, before making certain decisions. Partnerships should be forged together by a conjoined belief system that all parties agree upon. For instance, the Bible tells us not to be unequally yoked. The phrase "unequally yoked" comes from 2 Corinthians 6:14 (NASB): "Do not be bound together with unbelievers; for what partnership have righteousness and lawlessness, or what fellowship has light with darkness?"

A yoke is a wooden bar that joins two oxen to each other and to the burden they pull. An "unequally yoked" team has one stronger ox and one weaker, or two oxen that are not equivalent in size or stature. The weaker or smaller ox would walk more slowly than the larger, stronger one, causing them to walk and carry the load in circles. When oxen are unequally yoked, they cannot perform the task assigned to them. Instead of working together, they are at odds with one another.

The "unequal yoke" is often applied to business relationships. For a Christian to enter into a partnership with an unbeliever is to flirt with and eventually pursue disaster. Unbelievers have opposite worldviews and morals, and business decisions made daily will reflect the worldview of one partner or the other. For the relationship to work, one or the other must abandon their moral core and move toward that of the other. More often than not, it is the believer who finds themselves pressured to leave their Christian principles behind for the sake of profit and the growth of the business. This can all be avoided if we follow basic principles like connecting with someone that is likeminded.

Now, I can guarantee that there is someone saying to themselves right now, "What does a person's worldview have to do with them being a good partner?" Well, allow me to respond to with another question: why do so many marriages end due to irreconcilable differences? Is a marriage not a partnership? Doesn't worldview and morals if they are not in alignment with one another fit under the category of "irreconcilable differences"?

PRAYER

Now that we have this understanding, let us pray: Father God, we thank you for or allowing us to see our purpose and we ask that you ignite our passion that we can perform at a level of excellence that will be pleasing to you. Guide us in our decision making so that we don't make the mistake of burning unnecessary fuel, in Jesus' name, Amen.

_____

_____

_____

_____

_____

_____

_____

_____

_____

_____

_____

Chapter 4
HAVE SOME INTEGRITY ABOUT YOURSELF

Be a person that walks in integrity. To do, this we must first establish what integrity is. The definition of integrity is: "the quality of being honest and having strong moral principles; moral uprightness." So this statement is pretty self-explanatory, especially as it pertains to the next level. Yet, there is always someone who believes they already embody what it means to be a person of integrity, so this chapter is not for them.

It is for that reason that I will elaborate on the characteristics of a person with integrity. Some things that define such an individual would be treating others with love and kindness from a genuine place. An honest person, not with the intent to hurt the feelings of others with a brutal truth, but in a way where it can be edifying and beneficial to the growth of the individual while remaining in love throughout the process. A person with integrity strives to live an upright life behind closed doors as well as in public. Their heart's desire is to be unavailable to the enemy and his antics at all costs.

When you lead an upside-down life rather than a right-side up life, you become a magnetic force that attracts the enemy, allowing him to seek cohabitation in your life. When the Apostle Paul spoke to us in Ephesians 6:14, he told us to "put on the breastplate of righteousness." Today, we understand this to be integrity. We must be morally sound in our thoughts and in our actions.

How does this equate to natural life application? In business, there are two types of people we address: the crook and the good guy. Let's say they are both car salesmen and both want to sell a lot of cars. The crook is willing to lie to you about the quality of the car and tell you that there is nothing wrong with the vehicle, while the good guy is not willing to be dishonest to get the sale and he tells you the truth about the AC needing to be fixed. Sure, the crook might get the sale that day, but in the end, the good guy is going to get more referrals due to the fact that he considered the client's needs and respected them enough to be honest.

Which salesman would you rather deal with? I prefer the good guy over the crook. In fact, when it comes to hiring an employee, integrity is likely the number one quality that an employer seeks.

Well, how do you build your integrity, you ask? You simply decide to be an honest person, genuinely care about others, be helpful as often as you can, and live by a moral code of ethics. Your moral code should include but not be limited to things like speaking to others in a respectful manner, not having a petty or a messy nature that wards others off from ever wanting to deal with you, learning to lead a quiet life (1 Thessalonians 4:11) trying not offend others, don't be phony or unauthentic with your love and consideration for others, and consult the Holy Spirit with all decisions you must make (this ultimately should be the first thing that you do). These are some of the things you can practice to assist you on your journey to reaching the next level.

Chapter 5
LEAD BY EXAMPLE

This title says a mouthful, but in case you didn't get it in the first three words, I'm going to attempt to break it down so that it will forever be broken. Leadership is a quality that many people possess in some form or another. Some lead in higher positions at their place of employment, some lead in ministry departments at their church, some lead in school among their peers, and some lead in their homes as the example for their children. Truth is, there are even some people that lead in all of these areas at the same time. Being a good leader can prove to be difficult at times. That being said, it can still be done; difficult doesn't mean impossible. There are some leadership principles that will help you to become the best leader your arena.

First, let's establish that leaders don't decide to be leaders—they just are. People see something in a leader that compels them to want to follow. So, like it or not, you are most likely someone's leader. Now it is up to you to decide what type of leader you would like to be. You can be someone that doesn't care that you have a following and choose to live your life recklessly or you can choose to care about people and decide to live your life in such a way that inspires only the best to be presented in others. I must say the latter is the road to success, so if that's not where you want to go, then I urge you to put the book down because this read is not for you. Yet, if you are striving for success, then do yourself a favor and keep reading.

Some characteristics of a great leader are that they are honest, caring, genuine, and positive thinkers. They are problem solvers, charismatic, inspiring, attentive, selfless at the right times, confident, logical, self-controlled, and they think outside the box. Now, if you possess most of these characteristics, you are already great, but we must go further. Leaders set the standard for the group. If there is no order, that's because the leader is not organized. If timelines are an issue that's because the leader is a late bird. If there is a problem following the dress code, I'm sure you get the picture. On the flip side, if the leader is orderly, stern, kind, understanding, early, positive, and follows up with their team to make sure that duties are handled properly and in a timely manner, then the group will most likely be full of productive and happy people who respect and love their leader. This is most commonly the standard that leaders are to follow in community groups, churches, and businesses.

There are a long list of misconceptions that people have while they are in leadership positions, but I'm only going to highlight a few of them. One misunderstanding that some leaders have is that they are the boss and that others have to do what they say. In some cases, it is true that you are the boss, but it is never true in any case that people *have to* do what you say. In your workplace, people still have options. They could choose not to work for your company anymore because you don't treat them like they are a part of a team. This also goes for churches. The work that others do for a ministry is most likely on a voluntary basis and most people would never volunteer to be handled in this way. As leaders, we must try to maintain a level of understanding that encourages the best efforts from others and not make them feel like their efforts are never good enough.

Another misconception is that people don't need to be praised for something that they signed up to do. This is a huge issue for many companies and it ultimately leads lots of people on a quest for new job opportunities. It also leads lots of people on a journey to finding a new place of worship.

Chapter 6

BURYING MONEY WON'T GROW A TREE

In this chapter I want to talk to you about the thing we all want a lot of but most don't know how to manage: *money*. Now, I'm sure if you're anything like me you have sat through seminars telling you how to acquire it, watched videos on how to gain it, even read books giving instructions on what to do to attain it, but have come up short every time you attempted to apply these practices to your daily routine. While there are probably many reasons why it didn't work for you each time you tried and some of those reasons could be beyond your control, some things are in your control that you may not have applied correctly and most likely had the greatest effect on your outcome.

The first thing you must consider is that the earth is the Lord's and the fullness thereof, so taking it from Him is something that I'm certain is not going to happen. Now that we got that revelation out in the open I have some great news to share with you: God already let us know that He has no problem sharing His wealth with us. He says in 3 John 1:2 that He wants us to prosper and be in good health even as our soul prospers.

Look at today's economic society. Nothing happens without *money*. You don't even get recognized in certain circles unless your financial status is confirmed and "up to par." Look at healthcare: with money, you get the best treatment and without it, you get a Band-Aid and a trip home to sleep your ailments off. Money in today's world is how prosperity is measured.

Now, I didn't say this to make you angry at wealthy people; I said it to make you understand it is God's desire that you be blessed financially as well, but many times we stand in our own way of receiving the blessing God has stored for us. One major misconception that we have about how to gain financial freedom is that we must be tight or stingy with our coins, if you will, and that hiding away all that we have in a safe is the way to keep it. You are partly correct: that is a way to keep it, but it is not effective when it comes to making it grow. God tells us to make wise investments in Ecclesiastes 11:1-6. The Bible also speaks against those not seeking wise council when it comes to how to manage your funds in Matthew 25:14-30. So it is safe to say investing in businesses, stocks, and bonds are a good thing. Also, sitting down with a financial advisor could make all the difference when it comes to setting your financial structure. I know it's a tough concept to grasp for some, to imagine someone else having more knowledge on how to manage your money than you do. However, your money is no different than other people's money and God and school have equipped some people with the knowledge to handle and manage money. They are even educated on topics such as how to repair credit, and how to catch up all of your bills, and get you out of the red.

Next, we are going to look at how we should manage our money. The Bible tells us much about how to do this and the Scriptures apply in all aspects, even in economically tough times. Some ways to be a good steward of your money is to donate to charity (Psalm 112:5), create a budget and put away savings for you and your family (1 Corinthians 16:2), and clear up your debt (Romans 13:8). This one is a biggie; we need to steer clear of situations that imprison us with debt that is difficult, if not sometimes impossible, to pay back. Credit is an important factor to maintain in good standing because it empowers you to be able to make moves and get things done solely on the strength of your name and your word being true that you will return the funds in a timely manner.

Lastly, we must always remember to pay tithes. In the Old Testament, God makes a covenant with Israel that required the Israelites to tithe. The modern form of tithing is giving a certain percentage (ten percent in most cases) of your gross earnings to your church. While God no longer requires these tithes, your church needs this money to function. It allows the church to continue to do God's work in the lives of others, and one of the best ways to give back to a place where you worship and are being fed spiritually. Both tithing and giving to charity are things that can be used as a tax deduction as well, which is an added bonus for business-minded individuals.

PRACTICE FOR THIS CHAPTER

All of the things we have covered are things that we need to remember to spread the knowledge to the next generation. We sometimes get this information and work so hard to put it into practice, but often forget about the little people's lives that God has entrusted to us and how we are to lead guide and teach them the way to become independent, God-fearing, and self-sufficient. The last duty that we have as good stewards is to pay it forward. That is your practice for this chapter: teach your children or if you do not have children, mentor other children to find financial freedom and awareness. That, my friend, is what will catapult you to your next level.

_____

_____

_____

_____

_____

_____

_____

_____

_____

_____

Chapter 7
BE SILENT AND LISTEN

Have you ever noticed that the words "silent" and "listen" are made up of the same letters and much like their connection in the need for the same letters, it's also just as impossible to do one without doing the other? There are a few things you must do in order to "level up" and the previous statement is definitely one of them. There are also other things you must do, like pray without ceasing, study the Word of God constantly, let the Holy Spirit lead continuously, love others and God unconditionally, and practice having faith unwaveringly. This is not all, but it's a great place to start.

We want to claim all that God has for us, but we don't want to commit to what is required of us to receive those things. God has been consistent in the things He has promised us, even though we have done nothing to be deserving of them, yet it is us who show no consistency to God. We are hot one day and cold the next, seeking God and praying for others, then seeking personal gain and selfishly not considering others' needs, speaking life with absolute power and authority that God has blessed us with, and in the next breath speaking death and damnation over the same situation that we just breathed life into without a moment's consideration of what we have just done. We can be as inconsistent as it gets when it comes to the things of God. The great thing about God is that He is a gracious God that doesn't treat us the way we treat Him. In spite of our faults and shortcomings, He continues to love and protect us. Take a moment to imagine what life would be like if we got exactly what we deserved: *nothing*! Would there even be life? Because let's be honest, everyone has had a day that they did not deserve the breath of life breathed into their bodies, resulting in ceasing to exist. But that's not how God deals with us. He wants us to want to change, to want to be better each day, to wake up with a renewed state of mind, to seek Him in all things, and to live and choose our actions according to the guidance of the Holy Spirit. Sounds like a lot? That's because it's difficult to do with all of the temptation that the enemy places in our path daily, but it can be done—in fact, it has been proven.

I'm going to tell you a story about a real woman of God that I had the pleasure of knowing up close and personal. This woman is my grandmother Mary. To me and many others, she exemplified what a *real* believer and follower of Christ looks like. She dedicated time every day to acknowledge God in prayer and meditation, giving Him pure worship from her heart and soul—three times a day to be exact. She fed anyone that was hungry, and it was some of the best food known to mankind. It almost seemed as if she had prepared a feast for God every time she would enter the kitchen because every meal tasted as if God would even say "my compliments to the chef." She committed time to her family and loved ones, letting us know with every breath she breathed that she loved *all* of us. It sometimes makes you wonder is it possible to have the room for capacity in your heart to love so many equally, but she did it and we all felt it. She faithfully served at her church so committed even that she would walk to every service that the church held and get there on time.

She had so many other amazing characteristics that it would be impossible to sit and name them all. I'm not saying that she lived her life without a spot or wrinkle, but what I am saying is each day she awoke, she would make a conscious effort to be the best Mary that God called her to be and in our eyes, she came pretty close to perfect. She has gone on since then to her resting place, but I believe that because of the life she lived, she has secured a mansion in heaven.

Now, I didn't tell you the story of my grandmother Mary so you would get depressed and feel like you can never measure up to that type of lifestyle. I told you so that you may be inspired and encouraged to know that a woman born of the same flesh as you and I saw a need for a relationship with a God so big and mighty that she would silence her own fleshly desires to hear and obey the will of the Heavenly Father. The ability to do this is available to us all as well.

PRAYER

In order to silence your own voice, it will take much practice and prayer. Recite this prayer of affirmation: Lord, thank you for your continued guidance that your Holy Spirit provides. I ask you, Lord, to bridle my tongue and help me to understand when to speak and when to be silent. I speak in faith that I will listen to your will and obey, in Jesus' name, amen.

_____

_____

_____

_____

_____

_____

_____

_____

_____

_____

_____

Chapter 8
THE 3 D'S YOU MUST AVOID

Distraction by definition is something that prevents someone from giving full attention to something else. I believe that is enough reason in itself to avoid being distracted.

In order to be successful at anything there are certain times when your undivided attention is required. For instance, you want to start a non-profit organization and raise awareness to a cause close to your heart. You've begin doing all of your research, making the right connections, and seeking investors. You have not yet reached your goals, but you are making good headway. However, just as you are leaving another meeting with a potential investor and the feedback was not bad but not what you wanted to hear, you walk around the corner to the elevator and you overhear a group of financial executives laughing and insulting your business proposal, saying things like, "it was a poorly presented business plan" and "nobody cares about that cause because it doesn't increase the bottom dollar," or, "who would sign up to do business that's not good for business?"

You don't address them and you try to shrug it off, but when you get home and things settle down for the day, you begin to think about the rude insensitive statements they made. So much that it leads you to the second D you should avoid: Discouragement. You didn't get any sleep that night because you couldn't stop replaying their words in your mind. Eventually, you begin to question whether their words had merit. You even begin questioning the design of your program and whether or not it could work. You start to doubt that the idea is coming forth in its proper season. This is where the enemy can play with your vision because right now it's all a blurry. That voice of discouragement begins to speak to you, causing you to become confused and doubtful about a thing you were once sure of.

You worry, doubt, doubt and worry, until you step right into the third and final D to avoid: Defeat. Allowing what others have said or will say about your steps toward success to become the center of your attention will most definitely lead to the death of your vision. It can feel overwhelmingly difficult to fight their words off, but it can be done. In fact, it has been done many times. Don't just take my word for it. Ask any businessowner if they had to overcome these struggles. I can almost guarantee you that the answer is yes. Maybe it wasn't on the same level as the example or maybe it was in a worse situation than the example, but the outcome will be the same.

In order for the business to be successful, you will certainly hit this wall and it is all up to you whether you will have the strength to climb it or retreat back to your starting point.

PRAYER

As someone who knows this experience on a personal level and has had to ignore and forgive the words of outsiders, insiders, friends, and even family, it is my desire that you emerge no less than a conqueror in all things that are meant to steal your dreams and kill your vision. I release a prophetic proclamation over your life that you will not suffer defeat at the hands of distraction. I pray that God will center your focus and give you tunnel vision when necessary to achieve all that you dare to dream or imagine, in Jesus' name, Amen.

Chapter 9

SUBDUING NARCISSISTIC CHARACTERISTICS

I don't know if you realize it, but things just got deep and profound because we just entered the realm of psychological evaluation. Even though I majored in psychology, I am not qualified to diagnose anyone with any sort of mental illnesses or disorder, but there is much information to be found if you research in books and online on any particular subject that will give you a deeper insight that will be much more credible. However, I, with my acute senses and innate obsession to understand the human mind and all of its inner workings, am able to transfer information to you that I believe will be most beneficial to your successful advancement. Not only will it be a ladder for success, but it will also help you to understand in more detail the mind of the people you come into contact with on a daily basis, even those that you must connect with to get where you are going in life. It will become much easier to more smoothly navigate your way through life's obstacles and stumbling blocks.

While I do not personally believe everyone suffers from narcissism, I do believe most people have characteristics that are listed as narcissistic traits. In order to state this claim with all a certainty, I feel I must first define what narcissism is. According to Webster's dictionary, narcissism is defined as excessive or erotic interest in oneself and one's physical appearance. Yet, to truly understand the depth of what describes a narcissist we must go further. The more detailed explanation is someone that displays extreme selfishness, with a grandiose view of one's own talents and a craving for admiration, as characterizing a personality type. Narcissistic personality disorder, or NPD, is a real mental illness that, while clearly obvious to the naked untrained eye in many cases, should only be diagnosed by a licensed and trained mental health professional such as a psychologist or a psychiatrist.

Now that I have explained what narcissism is, I'm sure some of you are wondering what does this have to do with me being successful in all of my life's endeavors and how could this possibly directly affect me? Well, sometimes, more times than others, the things that go wrong in our lives are solely because we fail to plan or plan properly. While other times, our success, happiness, self-esteem, confidence, moral code of ethics, and yes, even sanity, can be challenged as a direct result of the company you keep, relationships we form, and even work or worship-related bonds.

Because this is such an important and relevant topic, I would like to take the time to dissect the examples given for each type of relationship and how they can be altered or dismantled by a person or persons displaying narcissistic characteristics. Please be advised that you may find the rate at how fast people with these traits will accumulate in your life, even in multiple areas of your life. My goal is to help you to understand the things that directly affect your daily growth, even the things that you currently are unaware of so that you can take the proper steps to remove all stumbling blocks, walls, and mountains standing between you and your destiny.

One of the most common and not easily avoided types of relationships that has the largest effect on your success rate is when the character traits are displayed through a loved one such as a family member or a romantic relationship. The reason for this is mainly due to the fact that you care more what they think about you and the decisions you make. We are taught to believe no one is going to want what's best for you more than your own family. Now this may be a true statement for some, but if it came down to a decision of them choosing between you and themselves, who do you think they would choose?

Themselves. While this is perfectly normal, what about situations where they choose themselves even when there is no comparison? This is where it gets a little sketchy. People with these characteristics have trouble identifying or sympathizing with another individual's situation, even if it is their loved one. They tend to internalize everything and make it about them and before long, the conversation will no longer be about you because they have reversed the roles.

For instance, if you are going through a tough time and you call that particular family member for advice they will either trump your problem with an even bigger problem of their own or cause you to feel extremely small by telling you how great things are for them at the current moment.

Another type of relationship that can cause you anguish is a work relationship. You can work alongside a co-worker that displays these characteristics and they will always be right, even when they're wrong; great, even when they're not; and confident, even when they're insecure. The overcompensating for these things will drive you insane. Let's say they are your boss. As your boss, they may take credit for all of your great ideas, attempt to outshine your personality so they can command all of the attention, abuse their position of power to control others, and not admit when they're wrong. If you're their boss, as your employee, they may seek sympathy from others just to discredit your managerial ethics, attempt to go above your head to the next ranking authority when dealing with issues, lie on you to get you fired, or dismiss any orders or directions you give them.

The last type of relationship that we will discuss is one that involves the spiritual narcissist. In most cases this type of narcissist is someone in a leadership position such as a pastor, bishop, elder, or minister because this individual thrives on power and control. They thrive on the feeling they get knowing that, in their mind, they are the superior being and that you look to them for guidance in your inferior state. They always have a selfish agenda and will be manipulating in order to get what they want. There is some twisting of words to confuse your understanding of Scripture or to compel you to give more money to his or her cause: them. I know by this time you have identified some familiar characteristics, whether it be in you or in someone you know but don't worry—there is hope for you to be able to overcome this obstacle no matter what side of the mountain you are standing on.

I find that with these types of topics, it is always best to refer to a higher authority: God. The Bible tells us in 2 Timothy 3:1-5 (NIV):

> There will be terrible times in the last days. People will be lovers of themselves, lovers of money, boastful, proud, abusive, disobedient to their parents, ungrateful, unholy, without love, unforgiving, slanderous, without self-control, brutal, not lovers of the good, treacherous, rash, conceited, lovers of pleasure rather than lovers of God— having a form of godliness but denying its power. Have nothing to do with such people.

Verse five is ultimately the best way to deal with these types of people, but it's not easily done, nor is it practical in the sense that there appears to be an alarming number of people that we have no choice but to encounter and it's ever increasing in epic proportions. It's even becoming more evident in our family and loved ones. These characteristics are becoming the new normal, whether it be our bosses, pastors, political leaders, doctors, lawyers, practically any profession or position that is undeniably vital to the functionality our everyday lives.

So what do you do to maintain your sanity and keep your focus? The first thing is you don't argue with them. Why? Well, for starters, you can't win an argument with someone that's not even listening to you. People that are conceited or proud find it hard to hear another person's views—especially if that view doesn't line up with their own. The next thing to remember is to have a limit that you won't go beyond. What this means is to be kind and cordial, but don't offer too much advice or personal information because it will only result in being used against you later. Your words will be twisted and used out of context, which will only cause you to get angry, act out of character, and appear irrational, which further makes the person with the narcissistic characteristics look even more normal and that much more believable. Stand your ground firmly, knowing your weakness and uncertainty gives them strength. After all, this is an issue of self-proclaimed superiority and grandeur. Don't expect explanations or apologies because they come few and far between. If in fact you do receive one, just know there is a self-serving motive behind the false sense of humility they express.

The last and perhaps the most important thing I want to convey to you is to keep reminding yourself to display genuine grace and compassion for all mankind, understanding there are many people that are this way, not just because they choose to take on these characteristics, but because they have a mental disorder that they cannot control. I'm sure there is a select group of people that display these characteristics but would rather not. They would give anything to feel compassion for others, or put someone else's needs before their own at least once in their lifetime. It's possible that some have had traumatic incidents occur in their youth that caused them to shut down emotionally or to go into self-preservation mode. If you are a believer of Christ, then you know the Word of God says "with love and kindness have I drawn thee and that is the likeness of Christ that we are to portray to the world"—yes, even the narcissist.

PRAYER

While this is a difficult thing to ask of anyone, it is not impossible. Therefore, I would like to pair my faith with yours in this moment to signify the triumphant victory that is to come. God, we bless your holy name for all things, and we ask that your understanding and forgiving spirit be displayed through us, just as it has been displayed to us, in your Son Jesus' name, Amen.

_____

_____

_____

_____

_____

_____

_____

_____

_____

_____

_____

_____

Chapter 10

G.O.A.L.S./ GREATNESS ON ALL LEVELS: STRIVE FOR IT!

How many times have you set goals and didn't reach them? Probably too many to count. When your goal deadline wasn't, met did you speed up to get things done as close to the deadline as possible or did you slow down or stop because you weren't motivated to continue seeing as to how you had already missed your deadline?

A lot of us have slowed down for lack of motivation. Don't feel bad; it happens to everyone at some point. The awesome thing is, you will be given another chance to succeed. And after reading and applying the information in this chapter, I'm sure you will do just that: *succeed*!

The first step to conquering this territory is to be determined to *strive for it*. Nothing that you obtain being worth something to you is going to come without a continuous effort or fight on your part. Some personal goals that you may have could be as big as being ready for the grand opening of your first business, or as small as finishing a new craft project for your house. No matter the size of the goal, the fight for the finish should always be the same: your absolute best. Let's take a writer that has a book deadline, for example. If that writer is not inspired, they have to seek out an atmosphere that gives them inspiration and focus on the task at hand. Sometimes, that is easier said than done. Unfortunately, at times, the author won't make the deadline that the publishing company set for the manuscript to be turned in, but do they stop trying? Not if they are a great writer and have a passion for what they do. They keep striving to get as close to that deadline as possible while still giving their absolute best effort to the project. This is what God is calling for in us. Do your best, not perfection. Proverbs 21:5 tells us that the plans of the diligent lead surely to abundance, so be diligent and continue to have plans and set goals, for it is rewarded with abundance.

Another acronym for GOAL is God On All Levels. If we are to succeed in life, we must remember to take Him with us on every level that we plan to climb. In fact, what's better is to let Him lead us through every level because He knows the way much better than we do.

One reason why we have issues when it comes to reaching our goals is that we may have trouble trying to balance all of life's responsibilities as well. For instance, you have a dream of being a great singer and you have a detailed plan of action to follow that came with deadlines to match. You have to write two verses for a project that you have been working on and then go into the studio and lay them down by the end of the week, but home life requires that you work a nine to five, drop off and pick up children form school, cook dinner, wash clothes, drop one child off to dance practice, one to guitar lesson, and one to football practice, pick them all up, make sure homework gets done, baths are given, and prepare to do it all again the next day. Do you see where this is going? I'm sure you do. For some, this can prove to be more complicated than for others. But, no worries! The answer is not far from reach. You must first pray and ask for direction. When you do this, you are inviting the Lord to be the voice of reason for all of your decision making. Doing this adds value to your plan because the Word of God tells us in Proverbs 3:6 to acknowledge Him in all of our ways and He will direct our path.

The thing that many of us don't realize is our Heavenly Father is looking for opportunities to bless us. He is excited about the times when we allow Him to rule in our lives because it gives Him a chance to flex His muscles and show us how strong He is.

After we have consulted with God about His plan for us, then we must prioritize our steps to reaching our desired goal. Don't worry—the Holy Spirit will help with this part as well. While it is good to exercise the brain muscles, it is better to write your plan out so you will have a reference point. After all, the Bible tells us to write the vision and make it plain.

Set the plan up in short term goals and long term goals because that makes it easier to track your progress. This is where the fruit of the spirit come into play. Once we have prayed, listened, prioritized, and written, we must be patient and wait for the right time to move forward. This part is difficult for most of us because by this time, we have become excited about the process, we've seen it on paper, and we prayed and trusted God, so now we are expecting to see miracles, signs, and wonders unfold, because God's word will not return to Him void. He tells us that though it tarry, wait for it, for it will come to pass. We are impatient beings by nature; it is our cross to bear, we must learn how to be patient.

I'm not saying you should sit down while you wait. Gather information, build resources and finances, consult with experts on the subject, and most importantly, worship while you wait. Waiting is inevitable—otherwise you run the risk of having a setback, which could cause you to have to wait even longer than originally projected. When we follow our God-given instinct and ability while trusting our guide, the Holy Spirit, the entire way, that's a recipe for greatness. There are many different paths we all take to get where we are going in life, but all are customized specifically with each one of us in mind and that's what makes our journey unique and what makes our story great: when we follow the storyline that the author created for us.

Chapter 11

EXCELLENCE IS THE ONLY STANDARD!

What does this mean? Colossians 3:23 says to "do all things as unto God and not man, knowing that your true reward comes for God." Now, does this mean God needs us to fulfill His work? No, because God is self-sufficient—in fact He is the filler of all of our needs as well, so having need of our works is just not possible for God. What it does convey is that God is calling us to a more excellent way of living that we may know the true rewards and benefits to His grace and joy.

Now, what does it mean to do *all things* in excellence? Clearly, every act in our lives is not a spiritual act, and God does not get the glory out of them all, right? Wrong. If God's spirit is within you and you are walking out your daily life's work, it is impossible for excellence to not be a part of your process of fulfilling your daily duties, unless of course you choose to exclude it from the process. For example, if you are washing your car and you go in and clean every nook and cranny, and you don't stop at just washing the car, but you also wax the car and shine the tires—that is excellence. You could have just done the basics and sure, for someone that would have been good enough, but it would not have qualified as a task fulfilled in excellence that would have been noteworthy and pleasing to all and it would not give you the satisfaction of God's joy as a reward.

Why do I say excellence is the only standard? Because if you operate with options on your standards, then you are liable to do what is easiest at times, in turn, causing you to fall short of God's glory, which is the ultimate reward of excellence.

We oftentimes choose to settle for what's less complicated, what doesn't make us try too hard—even the things that allow us to get by doing just enough, but with that, there is no reward, only completion.

Yet, a task done in the spirit of excellence will cause you to reap the benefits of a just reward, all while feeling accomplished, knowing you gave it your best. Some people do just enough to get by, yet they want to reap the rewards of a job well done. If you don't perform duties in an excellent way, then why would you ever have an expectation of an excellent reward? It's just not logical. On the other hand, when you do an excellent job, then let your benefit be the gratification of joy for your efforts on a job well done. On the road to excellence, some people will not like you or accept you because it's not common to go above the norm, but you can't let that stop you from striving for greatness daily. Just because you are working at it doesn't mean it's going to be easy. Let's just say the struggle is real. For anything worth attaining, there is always a dual force at work trying to keep you from it. It's up to you if you give up before the battle is won.

Yet, when you don't succeed, it's no one's fault but your own. Excellence is the thing that I must stress because it is a big factor in going to the next level. It sometimes will cost you relationships and that has to be okay because holding on to things that will hold you back will never allow you to develop excellence.

Now, you may feel like you have given it your best based on your level of expertise or based on the experience you have, but if that is where you stop and produce your work, are you truly giving it your best? I'm sorry to burst your joy bubbles but no—that is not what qualifies as giving it your best. "Best" is described in this situation as the effort you put into finding out all there is to know about something, and then applying even the new knowledge that you have just obtained to the duty at hand. For instance, if you are baking a cake from scratch and you know in order to make a cake, you will need flour, eggs, sugar, and butter, but that's all you know and you mix these ingredients together, take your cake batter, and put it in the oven, do you believe the cake you are making will be at its fullest potential, or even taste good, for that matter? Probably not. However, if you say to yourself, "I don't know all there is to know about making a cake," and look up a recipe, after you find out what it takes to make a great tasting cake, go and apply all that you have learned—for instance baking powder so that the cake will rise, vanilla flavor for a little richness, and measuring out all ingredients to the correct amount—then put it in the correct pan, place it into the oven set to the correct temperature, and take it out of the oven at the correct time, you will be able to feel confident in your outcome because you have not only followed all of the directions, but you have gone a step further to ensure you have done everything possible to have a beautiful product in the end, thus causing you to experience the feeling of joy at the hands of the excellent effort you made.

This same spirit of excellence applies in all areas of life, not just cake baking. Applying the same effort to anything will breed the same benefits of joy. For instance, on your job. If you get there on time, keep a positive attitude, and complete your tasks with an excellent standard, you may see some benefits like raises, bonuses, or even promotions. If you work in the youth department at your church and you set events and follow through with them, get to your meetings on time, bring new and creative biblical teaching methods to your youth, and do all of this in a positive spirit of love, you will see happy children that love to learn about God and parents that are proud to have work with their precious little people knowing they are in excellent care when they are with you.

Now to the juicy stuff. How do you level up and develop the spirit of excellence? You must first verbally affirm that you desire to operate with excellence as your only standard in all things. Then you must take every opportunity to apply more effort to your everyday tasks like getting up for work thirty minutes earlier than usual, or preparing for your day the night before. Now, for some, this is more difficult than for others, so you may need to place a note on your bathroom mirror to remind you in the morning that you plan to be excellent in all things today to receive your rewards of God's grace and joy. If you apply these principles and remain teachable, I guarantee you will soon know the feeling of operating in excellence.

Chapter 12
UTILIZE YOUR RESOURCES

This sounds simple enough, yet this is the area that we all have fallen short. This is partially due to the fact that many of us don't know what our resources are, so let me define the word resource: a stock or supply of money, materials, staff, and other assets that can be drawn on by a person or organization in order to function effectively.

Now that you have the meaning of the word "resource", I bet many of you are saying, "I don't have any resources." You may not have the obvious resources, but you are not without. The words "other assets" covers a lot. In order to know what type of resources you need and evaluate which ones are accessible to you, you must first have a goal in mind. If you don't have one or don't yet know what it is, that's okay too because that's where your first resource can come in handy: a life coach. I became a certified life coach for this very reason. I enjoy helping others to realize their goals and allowing them to come up with the best possible strategy of getting there. Having a coach can prove to be one of your biggest and most positive resources yet, they help build your character, self-esteem, and self-confidence. They also can be a great motivator to keep you morally grounded.

Now that you have identified your goal, you can begin to search for resources. Most goals that we set require money and other people's time, but we are not going to just deal with the obvious; we're going to go deeper. Prayer is a resource we take for granted on a regular basis. This is partly due to the fact that we underestimate the power of prayer. There are many Scriptures that support the fact that prayer is most definitely considered a resource. For example, I implore you to look at Joshua 10:12-13 when he prayed for the sun not to go down, and it didn't! God loves when we activate our faith through prayer.

Another stratagem we should recognize is knowledge. Knowledge is power and it is always readily available to access. You may only be able to go so far with free education, but go as far as you can go and I guarantee you that your hunger for learning will open more doors for you. Until then, make friends with people that are doing what you want to do so that you can glean from their wisdom and experience. Who knows, they may see something in you that will make them want to take you on as a mentee and possibly even be willing to invest financially in your vision. That's why being open to the plan of God to unfold in your life and willing to use what little you have in your hands is so important. It is vital that you believe in yourself enough to invest in yourself or no one else will. When it is evident that you forego drive-thru meals and eating out by bringing your lunch from home, and that you are resisting the temptation to go buy a new outfit for every occasion, instead you wear something you already own, these things are clear signs that you envision something more for your future and are moving toward it with each sacrifice you make.

PRAYER

I pray that your dreams become more clear to you with each passing day and that your desire to succeed supersedes your frustration due to lack of resources, so much that assistance becomes drawn to you like a magnet attaching itself to you at the appointed time.

Chapter 13
DEDICATE YOURSELF TO GOD

Dedication to God is a huge factor in the ability to live as a genuine believer. Just to say you are dedicated to the things of God is not enough, but to be fully dedicated is a lifestyle that a lot of people claim but not so many live out on a daily basis. Some may say, "See, I told you it can't be done because this sounds impossible to maintain" but that is simply not the case. Being dedicated is not about being "perfect" but more about being conscious of your shortcomings and willing to do the work to correct them. It's also about being able to ask God what He wants for your life and submitting to His will.

We must dedicate our visions, dreams, and desires to God as well. What do I mean? Well, I can tell you about myself when I demonstrated this act of devotion and dedication. I have been a cosmetologist by trade for over eighteen years at the time of this writing. My dream was to own my own salon. All I had was a vision and faith. I began to do research on what it would take to acquire a business legally. I became so engulfed in my research that I found myself hungry for information all the time. I even registered my fictitious name well before I ever had a salon because I didn't want anyone else to get my business name. I would pray constantly that God would bless me with a salon and I made a vow to Him that if He would do it, I would give it back to Him, much like Hannah did when she wanted to have a son by her husband even though she was barren (1 Samuel 1:11). I had a vision growing inside of me, just like a child soon began to grow Hannah's womb after God blessed her. I believed so much that God would honor my request.

One day, in conversation, I heard a woman was selling her salon. The young lady that told me about it didn't know about my desire to own a salon, nor did she know about the vow I had made to God. We were talking about other things and the subject came up. God has a way of answering prayers so you beyond a shadow of doubt that it was Him. She began to tell me how her mom was interested in buying this woman's salon, but she was asking for too much money and how it wasn't worth that much. Right then, I heard this voice inside of me (my guide, the Holy Spirit) say, "Go talk to her and see what she is asking for."

The next day, I met with the owner to find out some information from the source (also a great idea because we as believers make the common mistake of taking another person's word on a matter instead of going to the source just to find out later that we were given false or previous information that may no longer apply). The woman began to tell me what she wanted for the salon and I began to negotiate with her until we eventually reached a price we both agreed on. By the end of the conversation, she asked me could I meet with her that week to make the payment and that's when I informed her that I didn't have any money. She looked at me with what looked to be a mixture of frustration and confusion. I'm sure she was thinking, *why would you have me come down here just to waste my time?* Instead, what she said was, "When do you think you can pay it because I have to leave for California by the end of the week?"

I told her that I needed to break it up in payments and she gave me that same look, and said, "Okay, give me a little time to think about it and I will get back with you." I agreed, we then shook hands and parted ways. I was a little nervous about whether or not she would say yes to my request, seeing as to how she seemed to be getting the short end of the stick in her eyes. The full request along with all salon equipment and client records also included her leaving the lease on the building in her name and her business license attached to the business for one full year to give me time to build, and she would not receive her first payment until three months later. This was a little far-fetched, but God loves the kind of faith that believes in Him for the far-fetched things.

The next day I got a call from the owner of the salon and she admitted it was crazy but she agreed to my proposal and asked if I could come down and meet her to get the keys. This day, for me, solidified my faith in God. It assured me that if we believe, truly believe God for something and work hard toward it, God will honor our faith and good works and He will give us the desires of our heart.

I just had one thing left to do. After I jumped up and down, cried, praised God, and told my family, I then got my blessed oil and called my business partner and our prayer warriors and we immediately anointed every inch of that salon and dedicated it all back to God so that it would be used as a ministry headquarters to glorify Him and spread His love to the people. That became our first mission.

I often refer to my salon as a "coverup" because on the surface we do hair and beautify the exterior, but behind the scenes is a whole other force at work, spreading the love of Christ to each and every person that graces my chair and doing the work that's needed to beautify the interior as well. I cannot say I have gotten it all right or that I still don't make mistakes or bad decisions, but I can say when I realize I am off course from where God wants me to be or from where the Holy Spirit has been trying to guide me, then I will repent and refocus.

This is what we all must learn to do when we get off track: we must repent and refocus our efforts back to God's plan for our life. He is so gracious that He will give us opportunities to correct our mistakes. So now you must think inwardly, *What have I done that caused me to not be in complete alignment with the will of God as it pertains to my life and peoples' lives that are in direct connection to me?* Then, verbally state, "God, forgive me for the times I've gone astray and help me to refocus my efforts back to you." If you have done this, you have taken the next step to level up.

Going to the next level is not just about gains that are visible to the eye, but it is also about seeing where you are inside and advancing forward there also. I believe it's hard to gain ground in your spiritual self and not do so in your natural self, and vice versa. It may appear it can be done this way, but if you keep watching, in time, things will reveal just what's going on. It's also more difficult to maintain a beautifully articulated lie than it is to acknowledge the truth and build from there.

There is also another message in this story about my salon. I was listening to my worship music at work one day while having lunch before my next client arrived for her appointment and I heard the voice of God say to me, "In my obedience you will see my glory." It took me a moment to figure out what sounded like a riddle at the time. However, I soon learned the meaning of the message. God had said to me that if I walk through the door of obedience just as I did when he told me to go speak to the previous salon owner, there will be another door, the door of opportunity, waiting on the other side of it, like when the woman agreed to my proposal. While to some this may equate to the case of a woman desperate to sell because she, for whatever reason, couldn't continue to run her business, and I just happened upon the perfect opportunity at the perfect time to make the most perfect deal of a lifetime. However, if it weren't for the unction of the Holy Spirit telling me to go, the wheels would have never be set in motion.

God says to us in Jeremiah 29:11, "For I know the plans I have for you, plans to prosper you and not to harm you, plans to give you hope and a future." We must give God His glory for thinking so much of us that he would map out our every step to lead us to our destiny. Most importantly, we must be willing to follow the directions on the map that He designed specifically for each and every one of our lives. Then we will begin to know the feeling of growth beyond our own limitations.

Chapter 14

DON'T BE A STATISTIC

Don't be that person that can't see God in the people closest to you. So many times people in ministry try to mirror the expectations of the people they are ministering to: "If I say it like this they will relate," or, "If I pause right here, it will give them dramatic effect." Yet, if we could just give out only what God has placed on the inside of us, we would be more effective in ministry. Doing this also frees us from the pressure of other people's expectations of us. Second Corinthians 4:16-17 says we have to know that the power given to us by God is more than enough. Those of you that are spectators, watching for the come up or downfall of others, waiting for the reality TV show spirit to break out in another believer's life, I say to you: make sure that you clean the lenses on your glasses so you can clearly see the manifestation of the Lord's glory all over their life. God is saying to someone, "Don't just be a spectator, but be a prayer warrior willing to touch and agree on behalf of one another's situation and be a congratulator when God does it for them."

Spectators are necessary because they become witnesses to the moves of God, but the way you can maximize your usefulness and potential as a spectator is to level up and believe. For example: in a movie, there are two kinds of extras—ones who just need to be on set so they can build their resume but they don't get paid, and the extras that may get a small speaking roll and they get paid as well as build their resume. Which one would you rather be? No one ever says, "I want less; please give me less." If you are doing an amazing job as an extra, eventually you will get a principle role and then you will need quality extras on your set.

Become the person/people you want to attract. Be what you want others to be for you when you reach your next level in ministry, sound simple? That's because it is. We just have a way of complicating things. Look at the person in the mirror and tell them, "Ain't nothin' to it but to do it!"

What's next is to figure out "how" to "do it." First, you must say it to yourself and then say out loud, "I am genuinely happy for others when they succeed." Say it even at the smallest of triumphs and it will become more natural and genuine. I know someone is thinking, *this is dumb, I am happy for others, so I don't need to do this.* However, the trick to jealousy is that sometimes it will sneak up on you and before you know it—*boom!* You're jealous of your neighbor and you don't know how you got there, or how to reverse it. This exercise is simply a reminder that we must always feel this way about others, even if it's not our time to shine.

Second, you must be willing to do the work. It is staggering as to how many people pray for things, believe in God for things, and even focus on things that they desire, but never consider working for them. This is a step that works in every category we face in life—whether it be spiritual, mental, physical, emotional, material, or financial. When you want to grow or gain in either of these areas, you must do the work. Looking at the thing you want, and verbally affirming the thing you want is important, but it is not enough. You must now begin to do what it takes to get closer to reaching your goal. If showing love is something that you are not strong at doing, then you can practice by being helpful and offering your time to assist others. You can set time aside each day to call and check on others, you can spend time with the elderly, and you can practice genuinely giving to others without any expectations of them to return the gesture of kindness. These are all actions that display love.

Sometimes people can make it difficult for you to show them love. Now, before I go any further, I want to remind you that it doesn't matter how difficult it is, we still must do it. We must prove to be stronger than the difficulties we face. You never know—what if your greatest blessing is in your toughest triumph? To love someone in spite of their blatant distain and sheer lack of tolerance for you is difficult. I will go as far as to say it even feels impossible to do at times, but we know that is not the case because the Bible tells us in Matthew 19:26 that on our own strength we will fail, but with God, nothing is impossible.

So, some people make it difficult to show them love by not returning the love to you. There are people bent on breaking you down until your virtue begins to tear at the seams. Their only desire is to prove you are not perfect and that you are flawed like everyone else—especially if you have managed to maintain a status of respect by others' standards. There is just one thing that they didn't factor or take into consideration: you never professed to be perfect and the thing that others respect about you is your ability to bounce back in spite of your flaws.

One reason a person would be this way (set on breaking you) is because ultimately they admire you, and your moral ground and stable footing causes them to have to address their own shortcomings, so ultimately it makes them resent you for it. This can be discouraging to say the least, but it is in these times we must begin to encourage ourselves by using our verbal affirmations:

- Luke 6:28: "Pray for those that despitefully use you"
- 2 Corinthians 5:21: "I am the righteousness of God"
- Psalm 23:5: "Thou prepares a table before me in the presence of my enemies"

The Word of God is full of encouragement to strengthen you when you're weak. Everything that we need to apply to our lives in order to not be labeled as a statistic *will not* be easy, but it is possible and what's more important is that it is also necessary.

I feel the need to pray at this moment so if you will please join me: Heavenly Father, we thank you for your wisdom and guidance and we ask you now, Lord, to endow us with the fruit and power of your Holy Spirit that we may be able to resist all feelings and behaviors that are not like you. Help us to be to others who you called us to be in spite of who others have been to us because we understand that it pleases you. In your Son Jesus' name, Amen.

PRACTICE FOR THIS CHAPTER

When you need a reminder of how not to be a statistic, refer to this chapter. I have a feeling that this section of the book will have worn out pages before long due to constant page flipping, but that's all right because that just means it's working for your good. Stay focused; there's more to come!

_____

_____

_____

_____

_____

_____

_____

_____

_____

_____

_____

_____

_____

Chapter 15

YOUR AUTHENTICITY REQUIRES YOUR ACCOUNTABILITY

No matter what level, we are all searching for our purpose, a truly authentic purpose for which we were created. It may be on a professional or career-driven level, or maybe it's on a spiritual level. No matter what facet of life we are feeling most connected to at any given moment, we must remain accountable for the levels and timeframes of the successes and failures that we reach. It is inevitable that the quality of the work we do and the pace that we set to do the work will determine whether we reach our goals in life. It is just as true that if we don't do the work, we will not reach our goals and we can't blame anyone but ourselves.

I know—there is always someone that was supposed to assist you with getting things done and they let you down. I also know you didn't even ask them for help, but when they offered, you gladly accepted because you could use an extra pair of hands and another mind to bounce ideas off of. It's not fair—why offer your services if you were not committed to doing the work, right? *If they wouldn't have offered to help, I would have set my pace more accurately to complete the task on my own*, right? *It's their fault that I didn't make my deadline*, right? Wrong! It's not anyone's responsibility to bring you success. It is solely your responsibility to go get it! And when that doesn't happen, you can only hold yourself accountable.

I want you to take this moment to look at yourself and reflect back to a moment in your past that you didn't meet a deadline, or a specific goal that you had set for yourself was not met. Now, I want you to look closely into the reasons why it didn't happen. Then ask yourself, was this something that you could have done differently? Now, the last thing I want you to do is acknowledge the individual that was most affected by the failure to complete the task aforementioned. If the answers that you sought ended with you, then you are doing an excellent job of holding yourself accountable, but if they ended with someone else in the seat of blame, then you have yet to come to a place of truth within yourself and my work here is not done.

We can sometimes confuse the words "responsibility" and "accountability" and mistake one for the other. Well, it is my mission to unravel the "ravelies", as my daughter would say in her making up of words, in your confused way of thinking. Responsibility is a liability and accountability is also liability, but the difference is that responsibility can be shared and accountability cannot. For example: you were a part of a group project at school and the project was turned in incomplete. Everyone in the group receives a less than desirable grade because it was the responsibility of the group to turn in a complete project, but the only reason the project wasn't complete is because you didn't finish the section of the project that was assigned to you in time. This is where accountability comes in. The group has a right to be frustrated with you because your lack of effort caused everyone to suffer and for that, you must hold yourself accountable. But that is not the only accountability that needs to take place, because since this project grade was going to affect everyone, then each individual had a responsibility to stay on top of each other, making sure everything was running smoothly and offering to assist if necessary to get the job done. Because that didn't happen, each person must own the fact that they could have checked with you since you were the only one who hadn't shown your work and they must hold themselves accountable individually for not doing so.

This is the part where most people feel they fall short. The reason for this is because we oftentimes find it difficult to "baby" someone, as we sometimes like to call it, through a process for which they are responsible. Yet, if we are honest about it, there has been an area, or areas for some of us, that another individual has had to "baby" us through and if it had not been for their nagging persistence in pushing us toward better, we would not have arrived there. So why do we feel like because we have reached the mountain top that we shouldn't have to reach down to help pull someone else up? There is sense of entitlement that we all have become accustomed to where we believe if we don't get it, then we must not deserve it, but I want to challenge everyone to look at it from another perspective.

For instance, maybe instead of saying if you don't get it, you must not deserve it, say it's *possible* that you deserve it and you just don't know how to get it, so let me help you by telling you how I did it. Seems like a response that others would be much more receptive to, don't you think? Now, I'm not going to tell you that everyone will receive that response and all things will be peachy, because there are other factors to consider. They may have pride issues, or they may not have ever had someone try to help them before, so they don't know how to recognize it as help, or this, and this is a big one, they may have had a lot of fake people that said they want to help and when they got bored with the process, they left them high and dry, sometimes in a worse condition than when they first began to "help."

This is hard to come back from, especially if it has happened to you more than once, but if I may take a moment, I would like to address the individuals who have been placed in this predicament and know this feeling all too well. Don't let the pain of your past decisions affect your future endeavors or your future success. That season has come for us all and I would love to tell you that we all make it out of this extended winter but unfortunately, that isn't the case. For some, this is the end—the end of trying, hoping, trusting, striving, reaching, even the end of caring, but it doesn't have to be your story. You have the ability and the authority to write the ending that you want to see. So get your pencil and paper, laptop, notepad, recorder, or whatever your record keeping tool of choice is, and get to writing your blessed and prosperous autobiography. That's just the beginning. Allow the Holy Spirit to guide you toward your happy ending, knowing that along the way, there will be some times that you will make mistakes, but don't be afraid to hold yourself accountable, because it is only there to keep you on the right path. Accountability builds and strengthens character, and character defines the authentic you.

Chapter 16

THE TRUTH WILL MAKE YOU FREE!

John 8:32 is one of the truest statements ever written. Jesus let the people know He Himself is the truth. However, we know "the truth" to mean many other things to us. For instance, when we say something harsh or aggressive to offend someone, the excuse is, "I'm just telling you the truth and you need to toughen up and take it." Yet, the reality perhaps is we just said something we shouldn't have said to someone we shouldn't have said it to and the truth is that we have no real concept of truth because truth is God and God is love. Oftentimes we are willing to give these honest perceptions to others and pass them off as truth, but we are not willing to take them when someone gives them back.

There is sometimes a huge difference between honesty and truth. Honesty is "your truth" and actual truth is "fact." I'll prove it. What's the difference between these two statements: "I think the reason that people don't like you is because you always have something to say about everything," and, "the Bible tells us to be slow to speak and quick to listen"? One statement speaks biblical truth, while the other slowly tears down a person's self-esteem and confidence. The part where the assumption was made about why people don't like you is the part that made the statement "your truth" and not "the truth." The moment that was said, the intent of the speaker was proven malicious. The Word of God says in Proverbs 18:21 that we have the power to speak life or death, but just be aware that the same words you speak will set the standard for your life.

For many reasons, we will withhold the truth, using it only as our last possible option, but I heard a wise woman once say, "Truth is not an option." It's a must! When it comes to not being honest about things, it could be a selfish or a selfless act; however, we ultimately find that dishonesty comes with a price rather than a benefit. It can and has already cost so many their relationships, trust, jobs, respect, and so much more. So how do you avoid being a dishonest person and allow your life to speak truth to all with whom you come in contact? You must first know the *truth*, which is Christ, and learn of His teaching, which is the Word of God. Next, you need to understand God is *love* and He is also *the truth*, then the delivery of truth will be wrapped in love so it is able to be received in love when it is returned to you. Now, this is not to say the truth will make you all warm and fuzzy inside, but it is to say when it is done right, it will stand above all emotions and prove to be what is necessary for growth and maturity.

Truth can be painful to swallow sometimes, this is why many times, the responses when it is offered are not favorable. Because of our ability to become emotionally affected by things others say, we naturally respond from that place of our feelings that was pricked with the truth. It's not a good thing to lash out at others because we feel challenged, but the truth is it happens and it will continue to happen as long as we have not mastered the art of self-control. Now, many people think that others should be understanding of that fact and not respond back to your response negatively, but if that were possible, then you would have never responded negatively in the first place. Tongue twister? I know, but the best way to fix this verbal mess is to go back and acknowledge your wrong and here it is—the big one—apologize! I know this is hard to do at times, but trust me, the freedom that you get after you realize your part is done because you did the right thing us unexplainable. Now the weight lies on the other party to accept your apology or move past it.

PRAYER

I believe we all want peace of mind and a harmonious coexistence. But we can't get that when we are living, accepting, and concealing lies on a regular basis. So for this practice of going to the next level, I want you to pray this prayer: "God, help me to be honest in all things, and to display your love in the process, in Jesus' name, Amen."

Chapter 17
DON'T BE SCARED

Fear equates to failure but faith builds foundations. Fear can, and in most cases, will stand between you and where you want to go. It is the most effective tactic that the enemy uses today to stop us from walking into our destiny. We say courage is the opposing force of fear but there is only one force that drives out fear, and that is faith. Courage can only be built by an individual's level of faith. Deuteronomy 31:6 lets us know to "be strong and of good courage, do not be afraid for God is with you and he will not fail you." This Scripture clearly implies your faith in God will empower you with courage. Psalm 27:1 puts faith and fear in the same verse as well. There are many more Scriptures that connect these two factors so that should assure you of how we are supposed to deal with our fears.

Let fear activate your faith, then it will become useful. What do I mean? Fear of failing can take you in one of two directions: one is to not try and the other is to go to God for your natural ability, which is limited and has the potential to fail you, to become supernatural with the added power of God's strength. The Bible tells us in Proverbs 3:5-6 to trust in the Lord and lean not unto our own understanding, acknowledge Him in all our ways, and He will direct our path. In this passage, trust equals faith. And when we have faith in God and allow Him to direct our paths, we are building a strong foundation for success to abound.

When my son Tysen was seven years old, I put him in little league football. It was his first year ever playing any sport, so needless to say, he was a little intimidated and petrified. He loved football, but he was extremely afraid of getting hit, so much so that he would run the other direction or just drop to the ground whenever he had the ball, all just to avoid being tackled. He did this in practice and in games. Naturally, he was made to play a position that didn't fit his abilities. He was *fast*! His coach wanted to play him as a running back, but his fear had him as a wide receiver. In little league, that's like telling a child to go play with the butterflies while the rest of the team plays the game. That way, they can at least say you were on the field. That was my son's position the entire season: butterfly duty. I, being the mom that I am, continued to go to his games and support his "team effort." I would speak words of affirmation to him. I even put signs all over his room with Scripture confirming the things that I would say to him, like "God has not given us the spirit of fear but of power and a sound mind," and, "I can do all things through Christ who strengthens me." I bought training equipment for him to get better, yet he still remained on butterfly duty. After football, I decided to sign him up for track and field since we knew he was naturally fast. He took his track spikes and wrote Scripture on them. Not because I told him to, but because he had begun to believe it. As I expected him to do, he excelled. His confidence was at an all-time high so his coach was able to convince him to try football again the next season. That year was epic for him and his self-esteem. He played running back and he was the team captain. His team won every game and he was voted MVP and the coach on every team they played that year knew who my son was. That teaching has shaped him into one of the most positive thinking, inspiring, influential ten-year-old little leaders that I know. He now enters into every arena in his young life with the mindset, "if you believe, you will achieve."

Another angle the fear cripples is causing people to stay in unhealthy situations simply because they are afraid of the unknown. I agree that the unknown can be intimidating, but in some cases it is a better alternative to staying in some of the current situations you may be living through. A perfect example of this is marriage, that when weighed on a Richter scale, the positives lose to the negatives by a landslide. In fact, the only positive you can point out at the moment is the fact that you have someone and you're not alone, and even that is a lie when you look closer because the someone you have is also had by someone else at the same time that you have them and actually, *lonely* is the way you feel most of the time—even the times when they're home. We can agree this is definitely considered an unhealthy relationship, but we all, at some point have experienced a relationship like this personally or we know someone who has. We have even attempted to be that beacon of light that shines on the friend or loved one that we so lovingly view as the "dummy that won't leave", but if we can step outside of the judgment seat long enough to look a little closer, we will see the reason anyone stays in their current predicament is not because they are lacking common sense, but it is due to the fact that they are afraid of the unknown, or as I call it, the "what now?"

Success is scary to some for that exact reason. Many don't know if they have what it takes to continue producing the thing that will bring them their success. I believe this is like the "one hit wonder" syndrome where a person believes they only have one trick up their sleeve and when it becomes played out, then, "what now?" I have seen this happen to some of the most amazing vocalists that I have ever heard from my hometown. You mean you've never heard them sing?! You probably won't hear them if you don't go to their house or their church because that's as far as their reach extends when their growth was stunted by fear. Now, some people can sing well that don't desire to be a professional singer, and that's perfectly fine, but there are some that eat, sleep, and breathe music. They would want nothing more than to be discovered, but they won't do anything to pursue their dream because they doubt their ability to produce hits and stay at the top of their game.

You have to realize everything is always advancing and just like you learned what you needed to excel on this level, then continue seeking opportunities to further your education so that you can remain current and relevant on the particular subject matter. This is how you channel your fear—be afraid not to succeed, so much that your will to succeed becomes stronger than your fear of failing.

PRAYER

If you are ready to level up and grow beyond the limitations that you have placed on yourself in this area of your life, say this pray of affirmation with me: God, thank you for allowing me to see the areas where I am weak. Please give me the courage to believe in my abilities and trust that you will guide me through my process. Help me to step out on faith and just do it! In Jesus' name, Amen.

If you prayed this prayer in all sincerity then you are well on your way to the next level in your journey! See you at the top!

_____

_____

_____

_____

_____

_____

_____

_____

_____

_____

_____

_____

Chapter 18
BELIEVING IS SEEING

We have all heard the saying "seeing is believing," but have you ever considered it in reverse? Well, I would like to challenge you to think outside of the box for a moment, but be careful because you may end up liking things out here where there are no limitations, and decide to stay. I can't be held responsible for how many more levels you will climb and demons you will conquer due to your newfound freedom, so proceed at your own risk! Think about this for a moment: what if it is possible for you to believe something before it comes to pass? Imagine if you could will something into existence. That's crazy! But wait, it's true! That would imply the power to succeed is all in the mind and that's exactly where it is.

Nothing—and I mean *nothing*—happens without first being a thought. Everyday life, what's for dinner, putting gas in the car, donating to charity—everything is a thought before it becomes a reality. The very definition of faith is believing something that you can't see. What's beyond me is that as simple as this all sounds, many people cannot comprehend it. Maybe that's due to the fact that their faith level is depleted, or just the mere thought of a thought changing my reality sounds absurd.

I'm getting ready to mess up some people's critical belief or lack of belief system with this one: when you think you can't do something, do you do it? *Absolutely not!* Why do you think that is? Because the power of what you believe is in effect. I know someone is saying, "I have believed for something and it didn't happen, so what happened to my belief system being in effect then?" Great question, and I would like to answer by quoting James 2:14-17: "faith without works is dead." When you truly believe something, you can't help but to take steps that move toward what you believe to be so. So believing is not just a thought, but a thought that compels you to do the work.

I want to also challenge you to stretch your vision. What do I mean? Look ahead because you can only reach as far as you can see. The farther ahead you can see, the easier it becomes for you to elevate above your fears, your doubts, your haters, and your limitations. Why is it important for you to be able to elevate above people, places, and things? Not everyone is capable of going where God wants to take them. I know that's a sad thought, but don't be afraid to let dead weight fall off as you rise.

Just like animals adapt to their ever-changing environment or atmosphere, God will allow us to adjust to the atmosphere as we gain altitude. For instance, the air is thinner the higher you go, but if someone isn't meant to go higher with you, then you can't force them to be able to breathe easy at your level of elevation. When people begin to feel short of breath, they begin to panic and we all know a person in a panic can be dangerous, because at that moment, their only concern is for their need to breathe. So they will do anything to catch a breath, even try to steal your air.

PRAYER

I want to encourage you and let you know you were built for success and that what God has blessed, let no man curse. I claim a blessing over your extended vision beginning at this very moment, that your faith will cause you to walk into your greatness, no one else's, but yours, and that we may rejoice with others as they walk into theirs, Amen!

Chapter 19

DON'T LET FRUSTRATION CAUSE YOU TO QUIT

This is a practical and obvious statement to make, it doesn't hold any less true and pressing relevance than any of the other chapters. What's even more interesting is the fact that I came across this subject matter in a way that is even more practical and obvious than the title itself. I was frustrated, so much so that I thought about quitting. I considered quitting on my business, my family, my singing group, my church, and even worse, quitting on myself. What strong people sometimes don't want to admit is we haven't always been so strong. In fact, at times, we have been considered downright weak—weak enough to contemplate laying in our bed of defeat.

Well, I was there and I had purchased a first class ticket to Quittersville. What had me wound so tight attached itself to everything in my world and proceeded to drain the life right out of each entity. I believed my support system was weak, even nonexistent at times, and it made me angry. I believed I worked too hard to never be able to enjoy the fruits of my labor, and that also made me angry. I felt undervalued and unappreciated by the people I gave my all to and that burned my biscuits. Before I realized it, I walked around with a proverbial chip on my shoulder the size of Mount Rushmore. I didn't consider this comparison at the time, but along with the weight of the chip, there were people attached just like the faces of the presidents that were carved into Mount Rushmore. People that I felt contributed to my then-current condition. I don't know if you know this, but just in case you don't, I'm going to let you in on a little secret: our shoulders are not meant to carry chips and they were never strong enough to bear the weight of an entire mountain. We will always crack under that type of pressure if we don't relinquish our heavy load to the one who is more than able to bare it: God.

What I would like you to do is take a minute of your time right here and do a self-assessment by answering these questions:

- What types of things have made you feel a strong sense of frustration?
- Was it something that you could control or was it something beyond your control?
- Did you have any part in causing the frustration to begin or to elevate?
- Can you do anything to make the feeling of frustration subside?

These questions are designed to make you look at your situation more closely and to evaluate your own personal actions and weighing how *self* can contribute to the elevation of frustrations. Now, I believe once we realize how big of a roll we play in our own dramatic scenes of the movie that is our lives, we will be more attentive to rectifying the issues rather than throwing more coals on the fire.

For all who answered the questions in the assessment and came to the conclusion that their frustrations have not been self-inflicted and they did not have any contribution to their level of aggravation increasing, I'm going to first suggest you look again, because while you may not have been the cause of your own frustrations, you definitely are responsible for how you respond to them. Your response is the one thing that can defuse or escalate your tense state of mind. Even after you have taken a second look at yourself and you still insist you are not responsible for your bouts with frustration, I have you covered. The Bible tells us in Galatians 6:9 that we ought not be weary in our well doing, because if we can just hold on, we shall reap a harvest in due season. To hold on means don't quit. It also tells us in James 1:2-3 to "count it all joy whenever you face trials of many kinds, because you know that the testing of your faith produces perseverance."

So, it's more than safe to say frustration builds character. We learn how to endure, be patient, persevere, and we gain points in one of the fruits of the spirit: longsuffering.

PRAYER

I want you to make this prayer of affirmation a "go-to" declaration between you and God whenever you feel like you may be on the verge of turning up due to a frustration situation presenting itself. Father God, I need you to grant me peace like a river in this very moment. Help me to respond with the wisdom of your Holy Spirit, that my actions may be pleasing in your sight, Amen.

I believe if you pray this simple, yet impactful prayer, you will make better choices in your times of frustration, and that, my friend, is how you stretch beyond your limits!

Chapter 20

FOR ALL INTENTS AND PURPOSES

"For all intents and purposes" is a statement often used in a practical (meaning skilled at manual tasks) sense, but the purpose intended for your life is almost always anything but practical. You see, your ability to do, be, or create something may possibly be just a talent that you possess, but not your purpose. It may even be in direct connection to your purpose, but still not be your purpose. The great thing about talents and abilities is that they are things that keep you active while you seek out your designated purpose. In most cases, your talents are things that are necessary because they could possibly lead you to your life's purpose. Intent also means you could be attentively occupied with something, that is sometimes the things not aligned with your purpose.

Now, someone might be wondering, "Why is my purpose so difficult to identify?" Well, we as humans often have cloudy judgment and we, many times, may mistake a talent or gift as purpose, but when it no longer feels like it once did, we get discouraged, bored even, and move on to the next thing. Yet, when it is your purpose, there is no escaping it. You live and breathe it. It seems to somehow always find its way into your everyday thoughts and actions.

Take my story, for instance. I'm a cosmetologist by trade, which I am skilled in the art of styling and growing healthy hair. When my clients come in, we discuss the direction that they would like to go with their hair and then after I assess the state that the hair is in, we go into implementing a plan of action that will best suit them. Now, there are days when that is the extent of our stylist/client consultation and then there are days when the client comes in, sits in my chair, and entrusts their hair in my hands, but not only their hair—they may be overwhelmed or distressed about something dealing with their personal life and because of the call on my life that seems to work extremely well with my gift to do hair, they are able and comfortable opening up to me and releasing all of the things weighing heavily on them. Because I have a clear understanding of my duty as directed by God, I give them a listening ear and only when it's called for, a word from God.

See, sometimes we may feel we know what's best for a person and try to force it on them, but all we seem to do in the end is frustrate them more and send them out to further discuss their issues with a person that isn't qualified to help them. That is why we must know when it is important to listen and only listen. When you have done what is required of you by God, you then know the feeling of walking in purpose. Purpose causes you to feel accomplished and complete.

God has given us all a purpose (2 Timothy 1:9). It's embedded in our DNA. The reason we take so long sometimes finding and operating in our purpose is because we oftentimes get busy doing something that we can function as, but were not designed for. For instance, if you use a shirt to dry your hands, it will work, but it was designed to wear, so clearly it is not functioning in the manner it was intended. The same goes for our lives. We can be taking pictures and operating as a photographer when we were in fact designed to be a singer/songwriter. We do this also in ministry when it comes to our gifts and our calling or purpose. I sing on the praise team at my church, but recently I have been working in the media department, which is strange to me because I have little knowledge in this area, but I am a fast learner and I noticed the church could use some help with this particular ministry. Of course I am learning quite a bit about marketing and I'm even starting to like the job, but that's just it: it's still just a job and when I am up ministering through song, it never feels like a job. It's a part of me. I feel the same way when I gain knowledge about God and I get an opportunity to share it with someone, so I believe it's safe to say another extension to my purpose is evangelical. I say that to make you aware that you can have more than one purpose.

If there is any doubt about your life's purpose and you want to know for sure so that you can level up in life and in ministry, I want you to think about your life over the last five years and write down the things you did because you were good at them and then circle the ones that you do because you love them and will always find a way to do them. Now, of those things, which ones can be used to glorify God?

PRAYER

Whatever you are left with is certainly in direct connection to your purpose, if it's not in fact your purpose itself.

Pray this prayer with me: Lord, thank you for the desire to know the purpose for which you have created me. Guide me, step by step, that I may fulfill my life's work to your satisfaction in Jesus' name, Amen.

If you did the activity and recited the prayer, then you are definitely on the pathway to your purpose.

_____

_____

_____

_____

_____

_____

_____

_____

_____

_____

Chapter 21
KEEP UP OR GET LEFT BEHIND

I believe with a book titled *Stretch Marks: How to Grow Beyond Your Limits*, I think it's only right to tell you at what speed you should develop stretch marks. I heard a preacher once say, "When the speed of change around a thing becomes faster than the speed of change in a thing, the thing becomes irrelevant." This is true in all things: churches, businesses, and more. We sometimes get comfortable or complacent where we are—we get *stuck* and are afraid to change. In this case, there will be no stretch marks because there is no growth and as we all know, stretch marks are formed when there is rapid growth. Let's take a woman that is pregnant, for example. At first, there is no evidence of a child growing inside of her, but soon you begin to notice her belly changing. Growth, in small doses, is taking place, but there are still no stretch marks. Then, one day, out of nowhere, her belly and sometimes other body parts appear out of thin air and this time, there is stretching to her skin because the growth came rapidly and her skin had to quickly make room for the excess weight.

Just like the entire process of growth is beautiful for a woman birthing an adorable little blessing into the world, the same goes for a believer that is growing spiritually and soon will be giving birth in the form of activated purpose. Also, an individual impregnated with vision of entrepreneurship will soon birth it out. Stretch marks are simply a byproduct of the growing womb. And yes, in this way, men can get pregnant too. Yet, many view stretch marks as ugly battle scars. "I struggled with my weight for years and it left me with these ugly zebra stripes even after I lost the weight," but the focus was on the wrong thing. They should be acknowledging the fact that they are no longer struggling with weight loss and that they are a conqueror. See, the way God operates is that He will leave you with a reminder of how for you've come so that you can be proud of your growth and feel encouraged to keep climbing.

There is something that I must address before we go any further: stretching is good before any type of workout, but if it is done improperly, it could cause excruciating pain. It could also put you out of commission for a while. For instance, you could pull and tear tendons and ligaments if you are not careful. That's why it is best to receive and follow directions from a fitness instructor that knows how far to push you and when it's okay to advance. In the spiritual sense, the Holy Spirit is your guide, your fitness instructor. He will let you know when, where, and how far to go. He will be setting the pace or standard, if you will, for your workout because every fitness plan is formulated specifically to each individual's weight class, heart rate, and endurance level. Now, if you push yourself too far too fast, you might speed up your heart rate at an over-accelerated pace and cause a heart attack. This is life-threatening and critical, and if you make it out of a situation like this, it may change you to the point to where you can't stretch too far or even work out again because you have become high risk. This is not the position that you want to be in naturally nor spiritually.

Now, in the business sense, the fitness instructor would be a mentor or motivational speaker that encourages you to take a leap of faith. Otherwise, you may never know what potential is in you lying dormant. They inspire you to wake up that sleeping giant of success and let him roam free. If you notice in the Bible, many times that a situation calls for stretching of some sort, restoration, or a move from God, occurs. Don't take my word for it—read Matthew 12:13 and Exodus 9:29-33. There are many other reference points that prove this to be true. Stretching in the spiritual sense requires you to speak life, believe, hope, trust, love, have faith, and pray through difficult circumstances to get to the place where your blessing lies. So the stretch marks are there to remind you of how much you have grown in the process. With all certainty, say to yourself, "stretching is a blessing!"

Now, stretching in the natural sense is not much different because it too requires the same actions of you as stretching in the spiritual sense, but the only difference is your perspective. Maybe your focus is not to gain spiritual growth, but rather, to gain financial growth. You may be wondering how this method can work for you as well. First, let me say that spiritual growth leads to financial growth because God is the creator of all things—yes, even money—but your focus should never be to gain all the money in the world without first learning how to maintain and manage the money that you already have. We will talk about that more in detail in the next chapter. However, there is an order to things and many times we walk into things backward and wonder why we can't see stumbling blocks ahead.

Proper planning and believing in your vision are the main two things that will give you the upper hand when it comes to starting a business. There are many more factors to consider, but always remember if you fail to plan, then you plan to fail.

PRAYER

If you desire to stretch more than ever before and you know it will take the supernatural power of the Holy Spirit to guide you in your stretching process, say this prayer with me: Lord, thank you for showing me what I must do to stretch beyond the limits to receive all that you have predestined for me. Help me to exercise and expand my spiritual muscles that you may get the glory for my triumphs, Amen.

www.ingramcontent.com/pod-product-compliance
Ingram Content Group UK Ltd.
Pitfield, Milton Keynes, MK11 3LW, UK
UKHW022222230426
12048UKWH00016BA/998